GRAVITATIONAL WAVES
EXPLAINED

THE
MYSTERIES
OF
SPACE

GRAVITATIONAL WAVES

EXPLAINED

RICHARD GAUGHAN

Enslow Publishing
101 W. 23rd Street
Suite 240
New York, NY 10011
USA

enslow.com

For Patrick, whose influence extends through a room as
gravitational waves extend through the universe.

Acknowledgements

Thanks to Ryan Behunin for his patience in offering incisive insights and,
as ever, to the staff at Cline Library for helping ensure access to quality information.

Published in 2019 by Enslow Publishing, LLC.
101 W. 23rd Street, Suite 240, New York, NY 10011

Library of Congress Cataloging-in-Publication Data

Names: Gaughan, Richard, author.
Title: Gravitational waves explained / Richard Gaughan.
Description: New York : Enslow Publishing, [2019] | Series: The mysteries of space | Audience: Grades 7 to 12. | Includes bibliographical references and index.
Identifiers: LCCN 2018018567| ISBN 9781978504561 (library bound) | ISBN 9781978505575 (pbk.)
Subjects: LCSH: Gravitational waves—Juvenile literature. | General relativity (Physics)—Juvenile literature.
Classification: LCC QC179 .G38 2018 | DDC 530.11—dc23
LC record available at https://lccn.loc.gov/2018018567

Printed in the United States of America

To Our Readers: We have done our best to make sure all websites in this book were active and appropriate when we went to press. However, the author and the publisher have no control over and assume no liability for the material available on those websites or on any websites they may link to. Any comments or suggestions can be sent by email to customerservice@enslow.com.

CONTENTS

A deer walks through the forest and makes her way to a lake. A wind blows tree branches; the water rises and falls with a gentle roll. Sunlight glints off the water as she drops her head to drink. The sharp crack of a twig cuts through the air. She raises her head, ears pointing and alert. A distant rumble shakes the trees, and the deer nervously trots toward the woods. But the rumble grows into a roar, and she is jolted off her feet as an earthquake whips the ground back and forth. Moments later, the ground settles and she jumps back to her feet, shakes her head, and walks into the woods.

Her whole morning was filled with waves.

The wind blowing, the water rising and falling, the branches of the trees sweeping back and forth, the sound traveling through the air, the light coming from the sun, the earthquake knocking her off her feet—all those movements, all that energy flying from one spot to another, all are examples of waves. Those waves all act a certain way: something is pushed out of balance and comes back into balance.

Think about the sound from a snapping twig. The twig is surrounded by air. The snap of the twig pushes the air around it and the "pushed" air squishes a little bit—it compresses, so the air molecules in a small area are closer together. That's out

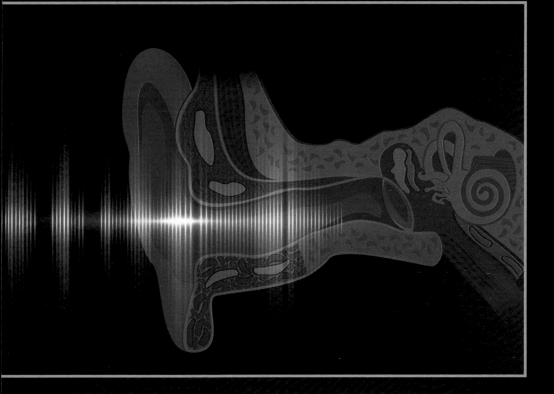

A sound wave is composed of traveling regions of high and low pressure. Parts of the ear move in and out when those high and low pressure regions move into the ear canal. That movement triggers nerve signals that the brain interprets as sound.

of balance with the air around it, so the "extra" molecules try to spread out and get back into balance. As they spread out, though, extra molecules move out into the neighboring area, where they make a new area that's out of balance. Then the same thing happens again. The result is a bundle of compressed and decompressed air that spreads out from the snapped twig. That bundle goes through the air where part of it is gathered in by the ear of the deer. The compressed and decompressed parts of the air push and pull on the eardrum of the deer, and she hears sound. Depending upon the sound she hears, she can make a decision about what made the sound, how far away it was, and what direction the sound has come from.

That example describes how sound waves start, how they travel, how they are detected, and what information they can carry. That same information is important for understanding any wave, but some waves are a little more difficult to understand.

Light waves, for example, travel across the entire universe, sometimes zipping along for billions of years, but there is nothing carrying them; they carry themselves along. But they're still created when something

Gravitational waves carry energy across the universe, traveling straight through anything in the way.

is knocked out of balance. And understanding them is pretty important because there's a lot to be learned from detecting light waves. Light can show when an apple is ripe. It can show how muscles contract. It can show how stars are formed.

There's another type of wave that is even more difficult to understand. In fact, until 2015, no one had ever detected this other type of wave, a type of wave that can provide information about some of the most dramatic events in the universe.

This type of wave is called a gravitational wave. Like light waves, gravitational waves aren't carried by air or water, but unlike light waves, gravitational waves don't travel through space: they *are* space. They carry information about space and the objects in space—especially very heavy objects. Detecting and interpreting gravitational waves leads to a new understanding of the strange and wonderful universe in which we live.

It all begins with one question: what is a wave?

Chapter One

What Is a Wave?

Waves are disturbances that carry energy. The disturbance is periodic, meaning it repeats itself at regular time intervals. The rate at which the wave repeats is the frequency. A wave also has a wavelength, which is the distance between one position where the disturbance is at its maximum and the next position of maximum disturbance. It also has a speed, how fast it carries energy. The speed is equal to the product of the frequency and the wavelength. Finally, a wave has an amplitude, a "size."

The Start of a Wave: A Disturbance

Imagine the surface of a lake on a calm day. The water is flat, mirror-like. It's flat because everything is in balance. In this case, balance means that every bit of water at the surface of the lake is "feeling" the exact same attraction to the center of Earth. In other words, every molecule on the surface is at the same distance from Earth's center.

The molecules are being pulled down, and they are also being pushed by the molecules around them. Each molecule is kind of like a person at a crowded concert. The person can't move left or right, backward or forward, because they bump against their neighbors. The molecule in the lake can't move left or right or backward or forward either. The neighboring molecules push back.

Now imagine one of those molecules—molecule one—gets pushed down to a lower layer. The lower layer was already "full," so molecule two below gets pushed to the side (panel A on the next page). There's no room there, so molecule three moves up (B). Gravity pulls molecule three back down, now pushing molecules two and four to the side. Molecule four pushes up on molecule five (C). All that pushing underneath the water makes it look from the top of the water as if a bump in the lake is traveling outward, even though the molecules themselves pretty much stay in the same spot (D).

The same thing repeats for molecule three. Energy is spreading out from molecule one to molecule three. And it keeps going like that. The molecules only move up and down, but energy is moving left to right. That description doesn't include all the details, but it gets the main point accross.

A wave is created when something is knocked out of balance. The balance for a water wave is created by the interactions between gravity and the molecules of water. Water molecules that move down push outward on the molecules underneath, which then push upward on the neighboring water molecules. The cycle continues, creating a water wave.

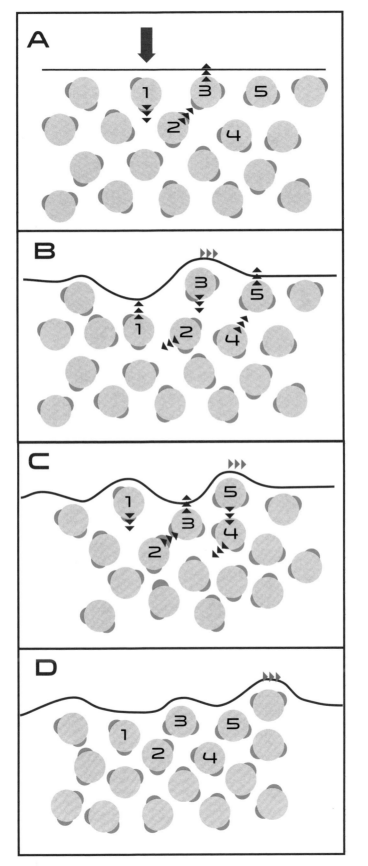

And the main point is that the disturbance carries energy from one spot to another. That's a wave.

What does that look like on the lake? It starts with a mirror-smooth surface, then a pebble is dropped in the middle of the lake. The pebble pushes water down, and the force of gravity works to bring things back into balance, sending energy out from the spot where the pebble was dropped. That up-and-down disturbance moves out from the center, creating a circular ripple that propagates, or travels in one direction from a specific starting point.[1]

Period and Frequency

What happens right where the pebble drops?

The pebble pushes the water down, where it's out of balance, and the water returns to its balance point. But it has extra energy, so it doesn't stop where it started, at the starting

Water waves are up and down disturbances that travel away from a starting point.

level of the lake. It keeps going above that point. When it's above, it's out of balance again, so it drops back to the balance point. But it still has extra energy, so it keeps going past the starting level and drops below. It's out of balance again, so it goes back up and the cycle keeps repeating.

That point right where the pebble dropped will go down and up and down and up over and over, until the friction among water molecules lessens the movement. The water always takes the same amount of time to go from down to up and back to down again. The time it takes for that bit of water to make one full round trip is called the period.

Instead of measuring how long it takes for the spot to go up and down, we can count how many times the spot goes up and down in a second. That's the frequency. Those are two different ways of measuring the same thing.[2]

Say, for example, the period is one-fifth of a second. That is, it takes one-fifth of a second for the water to make a full cycle from down to up to down again. That means the water would make five full cycles in one second; the frequency would be "five per second." There's a different name for "per second," and that is "hertz," abbreviated Hz. A frequency of five per second would be written "5 Hz."

We learn the period and frequency by looking at what happens to the water at a single point. We learn about the wavelength by looking at what happens to the water at different points.

Wavelength and Speed

When a pebble is dropped in the middle of the lake, the up and down motion of the water sends a ripple out to the shore. But now we know that the first up and down motion at the middle of the lake doesn't stop. It repeats. And every time it repeats, it sends a new circular ripple toward the shore. The distance between the top of one circular ripple and the top of the next one is the wavelength.

At any point along that wave, the water moves up and down at the same frequency as it does at the center point. And each time it moves up and down, that means a full wave has passed. That is, every period that passes means the energy carried by the wave has moved one wavelength farther. If there are five periods per second, then five wavelengths have passed by per second. So the speed at which the energy travels—the speed of the wave—is equal to the frequency multiplied by the wavelength. If the wavelength is 13 feet (4 meters) and the frequency is 5 Hz, then the speed is equal to 13 feet times 5 Hz, or 65 feet per second (or about 20 meters per second).

A STANDING WAVE

Mathematicians have a special name for a wave that doesn't travel. It's called a standing wave. When a guitar or piano player hits a string, they create a standing wave, for example. Something else that could be called a standing wave is when people in one section of a sports stadium stand up at the same time. Then people in the neighboring section stand up as people from the first section sit

(continued on the next page)

(continued from the previous page)

down, and so on around the stadium. "The wave," as it's usually called, has a lot of the same characteristics as other waves.

One of the most important features of any wave is easy to see in "the wave." No person in the wave is running around the stadium. Everyone stays at the same seat. Still, the wave itself travels around the stadium. The same thing holds true for every traveling wave: the disturbance is propagating but not the individual elements of the wave.

"The wave" is a disturbance that travels around a stadium. The disturbance travels, but no one leaves their place. That same thing happens with every type of wave.

Before moving on to understanding what can be learned from waves, there are two more important things to talk about.

First, think about what might be different if a big rock were to drop in the middle of the lake instead of a pebble. The rock makes a big splash and sends a larger ripple through the lake. The height of that ripple is the amplitude of the wave. The high point is called the crest or the peak of the wave, while the low point is called the trough.[3]

Now think about energy. Where the rock drops, the water goes up and down a certain amount—it has a certain amplitude. As the ripple goes out, the circle gets larger. There's no more

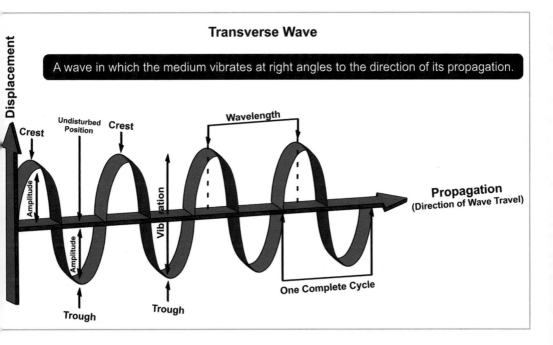

Transverse Wave

A wave in which the medium vibrates at right angles to the direction of its propagation.

Displacement

Crest

Undisturbed Position   Crest

Amplitude

Amplitude

Vibration

Wavelength

Propagation
(Direction of Wave Travel)

Trough

Trough

One Complete Cycle

Every wave has certain characteristics: the amplitude is the difference between the middle and the top (crest) of a wave; the wavelength is the distance between crests; the frequency is the number of crests that pass a point in one second; and the speed is how fast the disturbance travels.

energy in the ripple—it all came from dropping the rock—but the energy is spread out over the whole circle. Because the same energy is spread out over a larger circle, the amplitude of the wave gets smaller as the wave gets farther away.

Every wave has a frequency, wavelength, speed, and amplitude. Measuring those values can provide information about the source of the waves. But first, there's more to learn about the different types of waves.

Chapter Two

Getting on the Right Wavelength

Remember the deer drinking at the pond? She was affected by four different types of waves: light waves, water waves, sound waves, and seismic waves. Those waves are different from each other in a couple ways. First, although each is a traveling disturbance of balance, they are disturbing the balance of different things. Those things are the media they travel in, such as air or water, for example. Second, they disturb balance in different ways. They can squeeze forward and pull back in the direction they're moving, or they can push up and down perpendicular to the direction they travel. Knowing how waves travel is the first step toward knowing how to detect them.

Moving Along

The swelling ripples on the lake are nice examples of waves because everything is visible. What do the waves travel through?

Water. What direction does the water move? Up and down. What is the wavelength? The distance from one high point to the next high point. What's the frequency? The amount of time it takes the water to go up and down and back up again at a fixed point. What's the wave's speed? The frequency times the wavelength. What's the amplitude of the wave? Half the difference in height between the high point and the low point of the water.

Because everything in a water wave is visible, it's easy to see one more important feature of water waves. When a rock drops in the middle of the lake, a wave spreads out. The motion of the water is up and down, but the wave moves horizontally, along the surface of the lake. A fish bobber—a hollow plastic ball—floating on the surface will go up and down as the wave passes, but it won't move much left or right—even though the wave travels all the way from the center to the edge of the lake.

In water waves, the water itself moves perpendicular to the direction the wave travels. Those kinds of waves are called transverse waves.

Sound waves are a little different.

If you could see air molecules in equilibrium—another way of saying "in balance" or "at rest"—you would see a lot of little dots bumping into each other, kind of like a swarm of gnats zipping around the shore of a pond. Now take an imaginary box, say half an inch (about 12 millimeters) on a side, and capture all the molecules in that space. The number of molecules in that box represents the density of the air. Even though the molecules are buzzing all around, just like that cloud of gnats, the number in any box you grab will be just about the same.

A sound wave changes that picture. Sound pushes air molecules closer together so their density is higher. Those "extra" air molecules have to come from somewhere, and it turns out that they come from the space right behind the high-density region.

Think of a hand clap. When the hands are still apart, the space between them is filled with air. The air around is in equilibrium. When the hands come together the air between them is pushed out. The pushed-out air jams right against the air that was already there, which means the density right around the hands is higher than the equilibrium density. The extra molecules push against the air a little farther out, and the region of high-density air moves outward.

It's a little more complicated because every time extra air moves in one direction it leaves a region of lower density behind. Then other air rushes in to the region of lower density. A sound wave is composed of alternating regions of high and low density traveling through the air. If each air molecule were visible, like those gnats in a cloud, a sound wave would look like dark and light regions. The air molecules themselves move forward and back, in the same direction as the wave itself. That type of wave is called a longitudinal wave.[1]

The deer in the woods felt the water waves and heard sound waves through the air. She also felt waves in the ground. Waves in the ground are called seismic waves. Seismic waves can be both transverse and longitudinal. That is, some seismic waves are transverse while others are longitudinal.[2]

One more type of wave affected the deer: light waves. Light waves are something called electromagnetic radiation. Light, and other electromagnetic radiation, is not a disturbance in water, air, or ground. Electromagnetic radiation is a disturbance in itself.

LONGITUDINAL WAVES

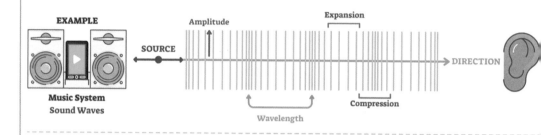

EXAMPLE

SOURCE

Amplitude

Expansion

DIRECTION

Music System
Sound Waves

Compression

Wavelength

TRANSVERSE WAVES

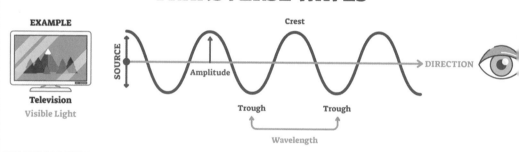

EXAMPLE

SOURCE

Crest

Amplitude

DIRECTION

Television
Visible Light

Trough

Trough

Wavelength

The disturbance in a longitudinal wave is back and forth in the same direction as the wave travels, while the disturbance in a transverse wave is perpendicular to the direction of travel.

Waves in Nothing

That's a strange thing to say, and maybe a little stranger to understand. It was just as strange for scientists to understand when they made observations and performed experiments in the late 1800s. Water waves move through water. Sound waves move through air. So electromagnetic waves must move through *something*. They called that something the "ether." They searched for the ether, but they never found it.

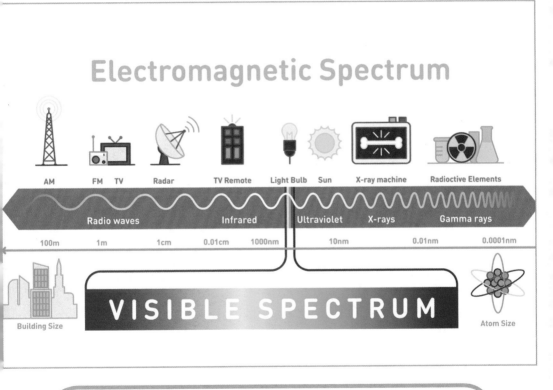

Light waves are just one type of electromagnetic radiation. Radio waves, X-rays, and microwaves are all just like light, except with different wavelengths.

NO ETHER HERE

Let's say Parker and Daneicia are both sailing on the lake when a fish leaps and crashes down, disturbing the balance and creating a wave. They decide to measure how fast the wave is traveling. Parker is sailing toward the fish's jump; Daneicia is sailing away from the wave's center. Parker sees the wave take two seconds to travel 2 yards (a little more than 1.75 meters). Daneicia measures six seconds for the wave to travel two yards along the side of her boat. The measured speeds are different because Parker and Daneicia are moving at different speeds on the medium, the water.

Scientists did that same experiment to detect the ether. They measured the speed of light at the time of year when Earth was headed toward the star Regulus, for example, then measured it again six months later, when Earth was in the part of its orbit that takes it away from Regulus. When Parker and Daniecia were moving in opposite directions, the water wave speed was different. The speed of light stayed the same for every measurement. Electromagnetic waves were not traveling like water waves on a lake—there was no ether.[3]

The dashed lines represent the line of sight of someone on Earth. In late summer, the observer is looking in the same direction as Earth is moving (toward Regulus). In early winter, the observer is looking opposite to Earth's motion (away from Regulus). If there were an ether, the speed of light would be different at each time of year. There is no difference, so there is no ether.

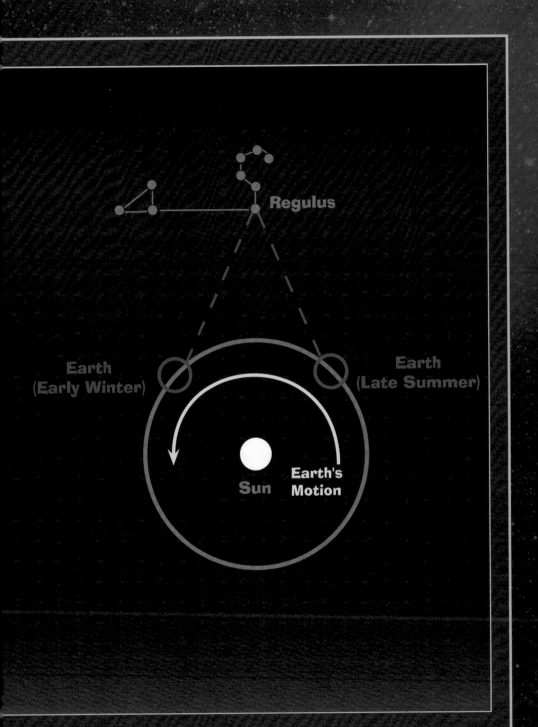

Before we can understand that, we need to know how electromagnetic waves are started. Radio waves, X-rays, microwaves, and light waves are each different types of electromagnetic radiation. All these types of electromagnetic radiation work according to the same principles, so let's look at a light wave.

Atoms are made up of heavy, positively charged centers called nuclei (one is called a nucleus, and the plural of nucleus is nuclei, pronounced "nuke-lee-eye"). Tiny, light, negatively charged particles whiz around the nucleus of an atom. Those negatively charged particles are electrons.

Electrons are much lighter than nuclei, so when outside forces interact with the atoms, most of the interaction is with the electrons. It's as if you had a basket full of marbles, each attached to a few feathers with a rubber band. If a wind blows, the marbles will move a little. The feathers, however, will jump and dance around at the end of their rubber bands. When the wind stops, the rubber bands will pull the feathers back toward their marbles. That's something like an atom.

Atoms feel forces from being bumped around—when you rub your hands together, for example, the warmth you feel is from atoms bumping into one another. Because atoms have positively and negatively charged particles they also feel other forces, including the force due to an electric field. Charged particles, such as the electrons and positive nuclei in an atom, also create their own electric fields.

When a blacksmith heats up a horseshoe, the heat from the coals makes the metal atoms in the horseshoe bump into one another. But the electrons—like those feathers—will dance and jump around. Again just like those feathers on their rubber bands, the electrons are pulled back toward their nuclei. When

CARBON ATOM

Atoms have both positive and negative charges (from the protons and electrons, respectively). They move in response to electric fields, and when they move, they create their own electromagnetic fields. So when the charges are knocked out of balance, they can create an electromagnetic wave.

the electrons jump back closer to their nuclei, their electric field changes quickly. That quick change in the electric field throws things out of balance—out of equilibrium.

The equilibrium they disturb is not an equilibrium in water or air; it's a disturbance in the balance of the electric field itself.

It turns out that when the balance of the electric field changes, it changes the balance of another field, called the magnetic field. Then the changing magnetic field creates changes in the electric field. The disturbance caused by the electrons ends up creating a burst of electric and magnetic fields that travels away. It also turns out that electromagnetic waves are transverse waves, with electric and magnetic fields perpendicular to the direction of travel. Those electric and magnetic fields keep feeding one another. They will go all the way across the universe until they hit something.

If the "something" they hit can detect light, then the information in the light can provide details about where it came from. Eventually, we'd like to do the same thing with gravitational waves: collect the information they carry. We can get clues about how to do that by investigating how we get information from other waves.

Learning from Waves

Waves carry information, but there's no way to get that information without first detecting the wave. Each type of wave needs a different type of detector. Each type of wave carries unique information. The "carrying" is the important point, since varied ways of detecting waves of different types provide insight into things happening far away. With that knowledge, it will then be time to start examining gravitational waves.

Eyes on the Wave

Remember those waves on the surface of the lake? They are transverse waves: the waves travel across the lake, but the water itself moves up and down. What would be needed to detect that kind of wave? The idea is to get as much information as possible about what caused the wave by measuring what happens at the shoreline. The water moves up and down, so the detector will need to move up and down as well.

A fish bobber floats on water, so it moves up and down as the water height changes. If a water wave comes by, the fish bobber motion would be the same as the transverse motion of the wave.

Here's one idea: put a fish bobber at the edge of a lake. Put a board behind it, marked with different heights, and have a big clock there, too. Point a video camera at the bobber and start recording.

The bobber would be at the same height when there were no waves, and it would bob up and down when a wave passed by. The height is the amplitude. The time between one wave top and the next shows the period.

Remember that the amplitude of the wave gets smaller as the wave travels. If the wave amplitude is, for example, one inch (2.54 centimeters), then that could mean that a small rock had dropped into the lake 50 feet (about 15 m) away from the

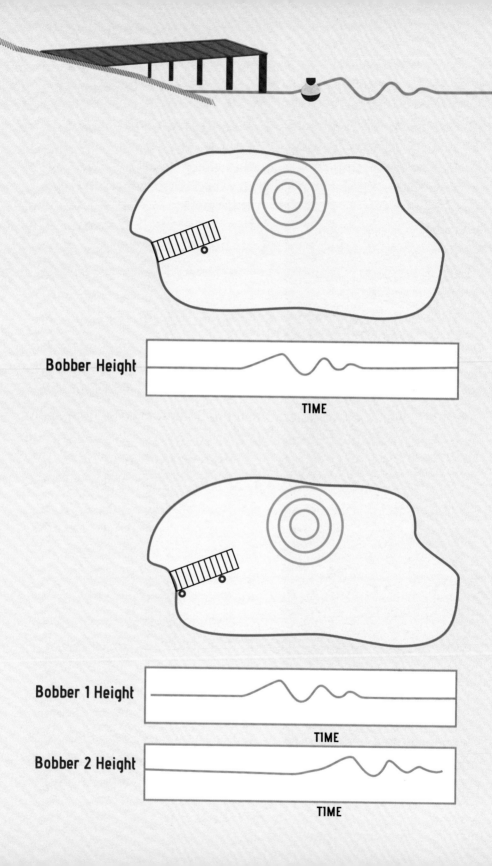

Bobber Height

TIME

Bobber 1 Height

TIME

Bobber 2 Height

TIME

A single fish bobber can detect a water wave, but it can't say anything about where a wave comes from. By looking at the timing of the signals from two fish bobbers, it's possible to narrow in on the source of a wave. The more bobbers there are, the more accurate the location would be.

detector. It could also mean that a much larger rock had dropped into the lake 200 feet (61 m) away. The bobber can't tell which direction the wave comes from, so it could come from the left or right or anywhere in between.

Another detector would fix that problem. If two waves arrive at the same time, then the wave must have come from a spot right between the two detectors. If the detector on the right sees the signal first, then the wave must have started on the right. If the time difference is larger, then the wave started farther to one side. Also, if the wave amplitude at one detector is smaller than at the other, that's another indication the wave started farther from one detector than from the other.

Those same principles work for detecting other waves, such as sound waves.

Sound waves are longitudinal waves. The regions of high air density push against the air ahead while the regions of low density kind of pull back. So a sound detector might look like a thin sheet of paper. High-density air pushes the paper inward. Low-density air pulls the paper outward. Imagine that paper is hooked up to a device that converts its position into an electrical signal. If that electrical signal is recorded on tape or in a computer then the detector will create a record of a sound wave. That's how a microphone works.

A microphone has a moveable membrane that slides back and forth as the pressure changes. When a sound wave hits, the membrane slides back and forth, and the position is converted to an electrical signal. A computer recording of the electrical signal shows the form of the sound wave.

Imagine the sheet of paper is replaced by a thin membrane of skin. Then use a brain to collect and process the signal. That's an ear. Using two ears, a living creature can tell the direction of the source of a sound. That deer by the side of the lake, for example, can easily tell the difference between a bird in a nearby tree to the left or a cougar growling from the woods behind.

That deer also felt the seismic waves through the ground. Seismic waves are both transverse and longitudinal, so more

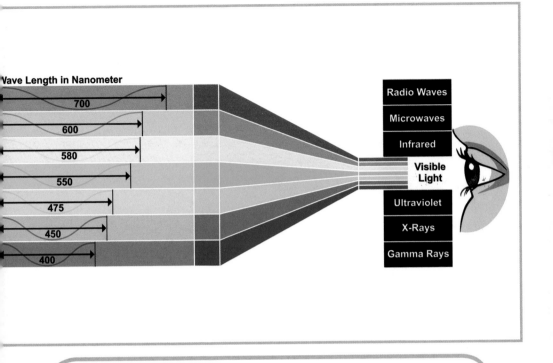

Wave Length in Nanometer

700
600
580
550
475
450
400

Radio Waves
Microwaves
Infrared
Visible Light
Ultraviolet
X-Rays
Gamma Rays

The colors of light indicate the wavelength and frequency of electromagnetic waves. Red light has a longer wavelength and a lower frequency than blue light.

than one type of detector would be needed. That is indeed how seismic waves are detected, by measuring the bumps and sways of the ground. The frequency and direction of seismic waves can provide information about where the waves came from, and they can also provide information about the ground between the source and the detector.

The deer also detected light waves. Light waves—electromagnetic radiation—consist of electric and magnetic fields. Those fields interact with positive and negative charges, so the detector will need to have positive or negative charges, or both. The back of the eye, for example, has molecules with electrons that react to electric fields.

USING SEISMIC WAVES

Oil—petroleum—deposits are far beneath the surface of Earth. It can't be touched, heard, or seen by anyone on the surface. How can explorers get an idea where to find oil? Seismic waves are one tool. Seismic waves happen during an earthquake—actually, earthquakes are groups of seismic waves—but geophysicists can't just wait around for an earthquake to happen. Instead, they set off a blast near the surface. The blast sends seismic waves into Earth, and some of them are reflected back. The waves reflect every time they reach a different material, as in when solid rock changes to a pool of underground crude oil. Geophysicists measure the time and direction of arrival for the reflected seismic waves. They use that information to construct a map of the hidden underground structures.[1]

Seismic waves travel through the ground, but they travel differently in varying materials. Because of that, geologists can measure the reflections of artificial seismic waves to figure out what kinds of rock lie underneath the surface.

Seismic exploration

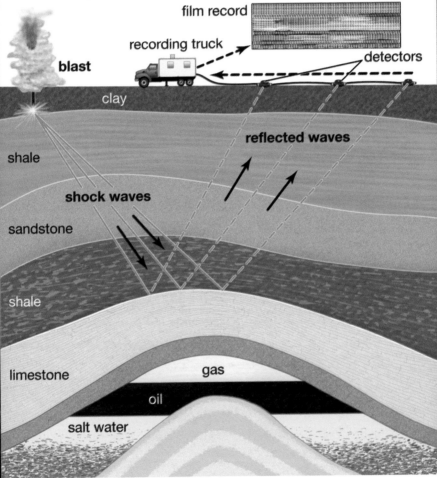

film record

recording truck

blast

detectors

clay

shale

reflected waves

shock waves

sandstone

shale

limestone

gas

oil

salt water

© 2012 Encyclopædia Britannica, Inc.

The color of the light indicates the frequency. Red light, for example, has a lower frequency than blue light. The brightness of the light—the amplitude—combined with the frequency can reveal light from a star at some unbelievable distance, a flashlight an arm's length away, or a patch of blue flowers across a grassy field.

Gathering Information with Waves

Let's go back to our deer at the edge of the lake. She heard the sound of the waves lapping at the water's edge. She looked at the lake and the area around the shore and saw nothing that made her nervous. Her ears, like her eyes, are very sensitive to the direction the wave is coming from, so she will have turned her head back and forth to see if there was anything to worry about.

While taking a sip of that cool lake water, she hears a twig crack. What information can she gather from that?

Her ears were pointed down to the water, so she is able to tell the sound of the crack came from behind her, but nothing else about the location of the sound. She knows the sound didn't last very long, she knows it wasn't very loud, and she knows it was neither very high pitched nor very low pitched.

The frequency tells her the sound didn't come from a bird singing or a tree falling. The duration of the sound tells her the sound didn't come from something running through the woods because there would have been more crashing and cracking. The amplitude of the sound doesn't tell her much because it could have been a small sound coming from close to her or a larger sound farther from her.

So what does she do? She turns to gather more information. She turns her head, aiming her sensitive ears behind her and directing her eyes to the woods. The lens in her eye focuses the light so that the amplitude and frequency at any one part of the retina represent a light wave coming from one specific spot. That is, the light coming off a green leaf high above the ground creates a tiny green spot at a specific location on her retina. She is sensitive to the color, the brightness, and the location of an object.

Her brain processes that information about the light wave — the amplitude, the frequency, and the direction of travel. She combines that with the sound she hears and creates an image of the world around her. Maybe she hears and sees a woodpecker tapping away high above the forest floor. Or perhaps she sees the tawny color of a cougar slinking along. Either way, she gets a new level of information that helps her decide what to do.

Humans collect information from waves to do that same thing. Information from waves tells us about the world around us, and the more information we can get, the better decisions we can make. That's one reason people are so interested in gravitational waves, because they provide information that's different from what we can get in any other way. But before we can detect gravitational waves, we need to know what they are.

Chapter Four

Gravitational
Waves

Gravitational waves are disturbances in the structure of the universe. But what creates the structure of the universe? And how can that structure be knocked out of equilibrium?

It turns out that the universe—space itself—is created by the matter and energy within it. That's kind of like saying that if a dark, empty room had all the air removed then it would not be there. Once matter is added then space appears, too, and the shape of the space—its structure—depends on what kind of matter and energy it contains. If the matter changes then the structure of space changes, too. A traveling change in the equilibrium structure of space is a gravitational wave.

The Structure of Space

In the 1600s, people had carefully observed the motion of objects in the heavens and gotten themselves pretty confused. From night to night, the stars were in the same location relative to one another. The planets moved among the stars, but they all moved at different speeds. Then there was the moon that zipped around Earth about every twenty-eight days. And how about the sun? Every single day the sun made its way all the way around Earth.

Thanks to astronomers such as Copernicus, Galileo, Tycho Brahe, and Johannes Kepler, people had a pretty good idea that

This illustration from the star atlas titled *Harmonia Macrocosmica* by Dutch-German cartographer Andreas Cellarius shows a heliocentric model of the universe. In the 1500s, Nicolaus Copernicus proposed that the planets orbited the sun, which was a change from the previous belief that everything in the universe circled around Earth.

the sun was at the center of rotation of all the planets, including Earth. That is, they had figured out that all the planets circled around the sun and that the moon circled around Earth. The stars? Well, they just seemed to hang out and not go anywhere.

So they had that model to work from, but they didn't know why any of that should be. Why, for example, did the moon circle Earth while all the other planets seemed to circle the sun? With all that mishmash of different motions there was one big question: what rules described the motion of objects in the sky?

Isaac Newton (1643–1727) cleared that up with one simple idea. Newton said the rules that governed motions in the heavens were the same as those that described motions of objects on Earth.

Newton saw apples fall from trees in his garden and he thought about what would happen if the apple trees were twice as tall. The apples would still fall straight down. What if the trees were ten times as tall? He still expected the apples to fall straight down. What if a tree was so tall that is stretched to the moon? He would still expect the apple to fall straight to the ground. So what about the moon, then; shouldn't it fall to Earth?

Newton realized that the moon *was* falling to Earth, but that it was circling around fast enough so that it moved along at just the right speed to stay at more or less the same distance from Earth. He invented a whole new kind of mathematics that let him describe the motion of the moon and all the other planets. His math led him to one simple idea: any two objects attract one another with a force that is proportional to their masses. That is, the strength of the attractive force is equal to (more or less) the weight of one object times the weight of the other object. Newton also realized the force attracting any two objects got

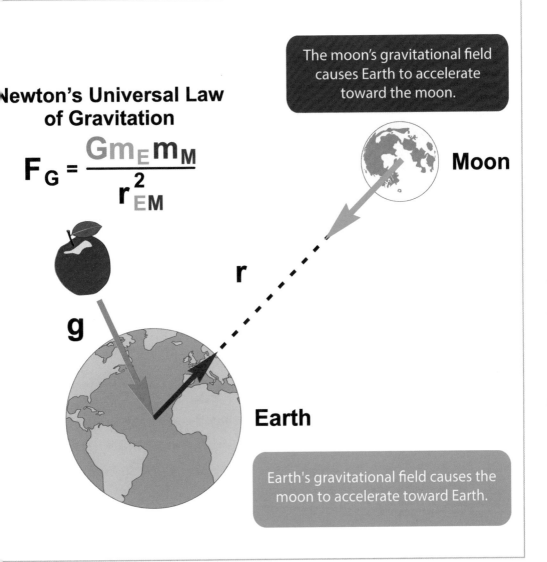

Newton's Universal Law of Gravitation

$$F_G = \frac{Gm_E m_M}{r^2_{EM}}$$

The moon's gravitational field causes Earth to accelerate toward the moon.

Moon

r

g

Earth

Earth's gravitational field causes the moon to accelerate toward Earth.

Newton's law of universal gravitation is responsible for the way apples fall to the ground and the way that the moon orbits Earth. This diagram illustrates this mathematical description of gravity where F_G is the pull of gravity, m_E is Earth's mass, m_M is the moon's mass, r is the distance between Earth and the moon, and G is the gravitational constant. The force of gravity between Earth and the apple is labeled g.

weaker as they got farther apart. In fact, if the distance between two objects doubled, then the force would be one-fourth as strong. That is, the force got weaker by a factor equal to the square of the distance between the two objects.

Putting those ideas together gave Newton an expression that described the motion of apples falling from trees, the moon going around Earth, and Jupiter going around the sun.

Newton's law became known as the law of universal gravitation because it described the gravitational attraction between any two objects in the universe. Newton's picture of the force of gravity between two objects is something like a rubber band between two marbles. That's not quite right because Newton's "rubber band" gets weaker as the marbles get farther apart, instead of stronger like a normal rubber band would get. But the idea is that there is some invisible line connecting those two marbles, so when object one moves, it influences the path of object two. And when object two moves, it influences the path of object one.

Newton's achievement was amazing. The math he came up with let National Air and Space Administration (NASA) engineers calculate everything needed to land people on the moon.

Newton was right.

But he wasn't quite perfect. Some tiny problems were poking holes in Newton's idea. Newton's idea needed to be changed a little, and Albert Einstein (1879–1955) was the man to do the changing.

Einstein's Gravity

The predictions of Newton's theory of gravity had proven themselves many times over, but around 1900, scientists had made some observations that didn't quite match. This was around the same time that scientists had discovered that electromagnetic waves didn't travel through some sort of ether. Einstein was about to tie those ideas together in a strange and complicated way.

Any time a theory explains a lot of observations, scientists have confidence it is true. But if even one observation doesn't fit, the theory isn't right. That doesn't necessarily mean the old theory is wrong; it's just not complete.

A theory that says cars always drive on the right side of the street would be correct—but not in England and some other countries where drivers go forward on the left side. For people in the United States, though, the first theory works great; it's just not complete—that is, it doesn't work everywhere.

Same thing with Newton's law: it works in many places; in fact, it works anyplace that gravity isn't "too strong." So where doesn't it work? One spot is very close to the sun. Mercury is the closest planet to the sun, and Mercury's orbit does not quite match the prediction of Newton's law of gravity. Einstein looked at that problem, and a few others, and figured out those problems could all be solved by a different understanding of gravity.

Matter is anything that could theoretically be touched—from an atom to a giant star, including things such as baseballs, kittens, and volcanoes. Newton thought of space as just a place for matter to hang out. In Newton's theory, if space were a tabletop then matter would be something like marbles or pebbles sitting on top.

After working through long and complicated mathematical derivations, Einstein realized that gravity could be explained if matter has an effect on space. In fact, according to Einstein, there's no space without matter, and without space there's nowhere for matter to be. One more complication to Einstein's theory: matter and energy are just different ways of looking at the same thing. So space exists anywhere there is matter and anywhere there is energy.[1]

CHECKING EINSTEIN

Every scientific theory is only as good as the data that backs it up. Scientists say they can never prove a theory, they can only disprove it. That's another way of saying that not every imaginable situation can be measured. For example, a scientist might see four students who are late to school because they look at their phones too long when they wake up. She could make a theory that phones are responsible for making students late to school. She could test it hundreds, thousands, millions of times. Even if every student she observed spent too much time updating their status on their phones, her theory would not be proven because the next student might be late because he took too long to eat breakfast.

Einstein's theory of general relativity is like that. So far, every test has shown Einstein's theory to be right. Einstein's theory predicts gravitational waves, but they're not easy to find, which is one reason why scientists were eager to build a detector for gravitational waves.[2]

If all the matter in the universe were evenly spread out, then all space would be identical—just like Newton's tabletop. But all matter isn't evenly spread out; it's clumped together. Where matter (and energy) is clumped together, space itself is pulled together. The tabletop is no longer flat. Instead it is pulled out of shape—it's curved—where there is matter.

In Einstein's picture, two marbles aren't connected with some sort of invisible rubber band. In fact, nothing connects them at all.

Newton's law of gravity was good, but it wasn't perfect. Einstein came up with a better description. In Einstein's understanding, gravity wasn't something that happened *in* space, it was something that happened *to* space. Gravity, said Einstein, happened when matter, such as these two red spheres, made space curve.

Instead, each of the marbles curves the space around itself. Two marbles that are near one another will curve the space around each other, too. When the marbles roll along the curved space they will go around each other, just as they did in Newton's model.

That curving of space is what makes gravitational waves possible. Which brings up the next question: how do gravitational waves curve space?

Chapter Five

Detecting the Barely Detectable

A detector needs to be matched to the type of wave it's trying to detect. For the changing height of water waves, a floating bobber works. For the high and low air pressure regions of sound waves, a thin vibrating membrane works. For the changing electric and magnetic fields of electromagnetic waves, detectors with moveable electronic charges will work.

Gravitational waves are changes in the structure of space. That sounds tough enough, but it gets a little harder because those changes in the structure of space are very small. The detector that's right for the job is something called a laser interferometer. The bad news is that it needs to be huge and supersensitive, and that's not an easy job. The good news is it has already been built, and it has already detected gravitational waves.

A Disturbance of Space

Go back to thinking of the universe as a tabletop. Imagine that tabletop is not made of stone or wood, but is instead made of knitted yarn, like a giant scarf. In a universe where all the matter and energy is spread out evenly, the whole surface is made of little knitted squares, all identical. Looked at from above, the tabletop universe would look like a sheet of graph paper, with straight

Earth and the sun are both composed of matter, which means they both curve the space around them. Earth's orbit is a path along that curved space.

lines from edge to edge. Anything that started out drifting along one of those lines would stay on that line all the way across the universe. The distance from one square to the next would be the same all across the universe.

Now imagine a clump of matter and energy collects together at one spot. At that spot, the little knitted squares would be bunched together and distorted. Looked at from above, the lines would curve inward close to the clump and get straighter with distance from the matter clump. In this universe, an object that starts out drifting along one of those lines will stay on that line. If the line curves closer to the clump then the object will drift closer to the clump of matter.

That knitted scarf represents the structure of space, but it's completely invisible. That little clump, for example, could be the sun. Earth, then, would drift along one of those lines that curves around the sun. There's nothing to see, but instead of traveling straight, Earth loops around the sun once a year.

Now imagine Earth and the sun have a universe all to themselves where they have been frozen in place, unmoving for all time. Call this "Snapshot 1." Earth and the sun are matter, so they curve the lines in the structure of space-time, and those curves stretch throughout the universe. That is, at some distant point in the universe, the square pattern of space is a little longer in one direction and a little shorter in the other.

Look at that same scene, but imagine Earth was frozen in a different spot, where it would be three months later in its orbit. That's "Snapshot 2." At the same distant spot, the square pattern is still distorted, but the direction that was a little longer in Snapshot 1 is a little shorter in Snapshot 2. The shorter distortion in Snapshot 1 is the longer direction in Snapshot 2.

Earth and the sun, however, are not frozen in space. They move. As they move, the pattern of distortion changes all throughout the rest of the universe. But it takes time for that distortion to travel through space. In fact, it travels at the speed of light.[1]

The moving Earth and sun create a disturbance in the structure of space—a wave—that is half a light-year (2.94 trillion miles, or 4.75 trillion kilometers) long. The wavelength of that disturbance is a half light-year. The frequency is once per six months. That is, at one location it would take half a year to change from one maximum left-right distortion to another maximum left-right distortion. The speed is the wavelength times the frequency, which is equal to the speed of light.

The final piece of necessary information is the amplitude.

For Earth and the sun, the amplitude is really, really small. Later we'll get an idea how small, but now it's time to think about how to measure a wave that is a distortion in space itself.

Measuring Changes in Space

Water wave detectors sense water height, sound wave detectors sense air pressure, and electromagnetic wave detectors sense forces on electric charge. Gravitational wave detectors must sense changes in the length of space.

A ruler won't work because space itself is stretching or compressing, and the gravity wave will pull or push the length of the ruler right along with it. There's one other problem: gravitational waves have a very tiny amplitude. A gravitational wave coming through the solar system, for example, would stretch or compress the distance between Earth and the sun. That distance is roughly 93 million miles (about 150 million km).

Gravitational waves distort space itself. A gravitational wave detector would pick up these changes.

How much would it change the distance between Earth and the sun? By something less than the thickness of an ant's antenna. In fact, less than one-millionth of the thickness of an ant's antenna.

It would be a little impractical to build a detector from here to the sun, so it will need to be a little smaller, maybe about forty million times smaller. If the detector is that much smaller, the distance change it's trying to measure is also that much smaller.

For a detector about 2.5 miles (4 km) long, a gravitational wave would only change that distance by less than one-millionth of a millionth of the thickness of that ant's antenna.

That's an almost impossible measurement.

And it gets even harder. Like the knitted squares on that scarf, when one direction gets longer, the other direction gets shorter. That means there can't just be one 2.5-mile-long detector; there needs to be another one, ideally at right angles to the first.[2]

So here's the job: detect changes in the invisible structure of space by measuring the distance of two different 2.5-mile-long paths and make the measurement accurate to less than one-trillionth of the width of an ant's antenna.

Scientists figured out a way to make that measurement. Instead of trying to measure the distance of those two arms of the detector, they measure the change in the time it takes to travel back and forth along each of those two detector arms. Say they had a little remote-controlled car, for example, that always took exactly two minutes to make it back and forth along one of the arms. If a gravity wave stretched the detector arm, then the car would take more than two minutes to make the round trip. A car traveling down the other arm would take a little less than two minutes because the stretch of the first arm is matched by shrinkage in the second arm.

The problems with that approach are first, that no remote-controlled car will have a constant speed, and second, the change in the travel time for that car would be so small that it couldn't be measured. Both those problems can be solved by replacing the remote-controlled car with a beam of light.

Light always travels at the same speed, so a beam that bounces off mirrors at each end of the 2.5-mile track will always take the exact same time. The accuracy in the time

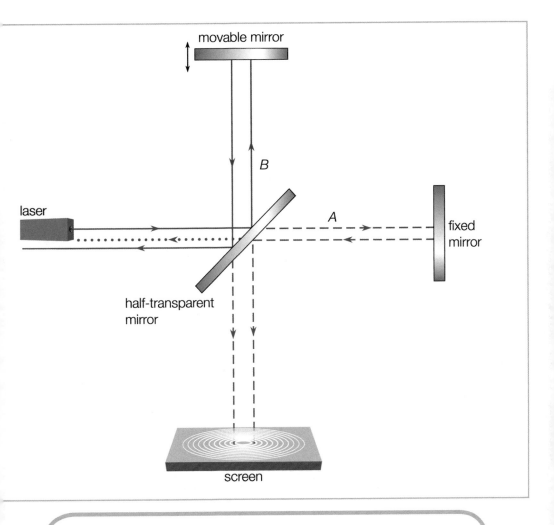

movable mirror

B

laser

A

fixed mirror

half-transparent mirror

screen

An interferometer measures small changes in distance between two separate light paths. The brightness of the two light beams together depends upon the difference in the time it takes for the beams to travel the two paths.

measurement is still a problem. It turns out, however, that two light beams prepared in the right way can make a very accurate time measurement. When brought together the two beams will create a pattern of a certain brightness. The brightness depends

TAKING A FEW ROUND TRIPS

A lot of work went into designing the laser for LIGO. When that light goes into the legs of the interferometer, a lot of it comes right out again. That wastes a lot of the energy. The solution is to do something called power recycling. The idea is to collect the light that would be wasted and to reflect it back into the system.[3] It's one more in a long list of complex systems that had to work to make LIGO sensitive enough to detect gravitational waves. Each time light goes back and forth between the mirrors in one of the LIGO legs, it has a chance to interact with the changes in space brought by the gravitational wave. The more light traveling between the mirrors, the more sensitive the detector. For LIGO, the light travels thousands of times along each track of the interferometer.[4]

upon the time difference between the light beams sent down each of the two different paths.

It is still a very tough measurement, but now at least it becomes possible.[5] The detector has two arms, each 2.5 miles long. The interferometer splits a specially prepared light beam so half goes to each arm of the detector, then it combines the beams carefully enough to measure a time difference of less than a millionth of a millionth of a millionth of a millionth of a second.

Researchers work in the LIGO control room. Similar to how the fish bobber detected disturbances in the water in the lake, the LIGO detector detects disturbances in the structure of space.

Not only did scientists and engineers build one of those detectors, they built two. They're called the laser interferometer gravitational observatory, or LIGO ("lye-go"). Even more astonishing, almost immediately after LIGO was ready to go, it detected an amazing extragalactic event: the crash of two gigantic black holes.

Chapter Six

A New View of the Universe

Before technological advances, humans could only perceive the world through their own senses. That works fine for things that are not too big or small, not too dangerous, and not too far to examine with touch, sight, smell, hearing, and taste. But the stars and planets are far beyond our reach. Galileo's telescope expanded the range of human senses and provided new insight into the objects in the sky. Ever since then, each new method of detection has provided new information that scientists have used to expand our understanding of the universe. The detection of gravitational waves now brings an entirely new way of gathering information about the universe, and it has already made an amazing discovery.

Ready for Discovery

The LIGO detector measures the length difference between two separate 2.5-mile-long tracks, each at a right angle to the other.

This aerial shot shows the two 2.5-mile-long tracks of the LIGO detector located in Livingston, Louisiana.

The system has been designed with two light beams, one to travel down each of those tracks. The two beams are brought together, where they create a pattern of a specific brightness. If the distance down one of those legs changes by even the smallest imaginable amount, then the brightness of that pattern will change. When the LIGO detector senses a change in brightness, it sends a signal to move a mirror to keep that brightness from changing. The larger the change in the length of the leg, the larger the signal needed to keep the intensity the same. By keeping track of that mirror signal, the LIGO detector records if, when, and by how much the lengths of the two detector legs change.

A lot of fancy engineering was needed—the laser has to be amazingly perfect, the mirrors have to be hung by tiny threads, even the reflective coatings on the mirrors needed unique stable designs.

Gravitational waves stretch space in one direction while they compress space in the other direction, so the LIGO detector is looking for that kind of length change in the two arms. LIGO's incredible sensitivity lets it identify those tiny changes. But maybe LIGO is too good. It is so sensitive that if a rancher drops a bale of hay in the fields around the detector then LIGO can sense it. And plenty of other activities generate local noise that masquerades as a signal.

LIGO also has one other problem. Remember the fish bobber on the lake? It senses the change in water height that comes as a wave passes by. But that water wave could come from any direction. There's no way that one detector can tell the direction. With a second fish bobber, the two signals can be compared to help locate the source of the wave. LIGO has the same issue: the changes in the structure of space are the same almost no matter which direction the wave comes from.

LIGO solves its two problems the same way, by having more than one detector. There are two LIGO detectors, one in Louisiana and another in Washington State. There's a slightly smaller gravitational wave detector, VIRGO, in Italy. If a haybale drops in Washington State, it might create a signal in Washington, but it won't create one in Louisiana. Eliminating signals that don't match in all the detectors gets rid of LIGO's problem with local noise. Comparing the times of matching signals solves LIGO's other problem. That gives at least a little bit of direction information about the source of a gravitational wave.

A Big Discovery of Big Things

In 1609, Galileo Galilei (1564–1642) built the most sensitive telescope that had ever been made. And in 1610, he observed the planet Jupiter. He found four small dots in the neighborhood of Jupiter—four small dots that changed their position with time. He realized those small dots were paired to Jupiter the same way the moon was paired to Earth. That changed the way that humans understood the universe.[1]

Almost four hundred years after Galileo discovered Jupiter's four largest moons, the Voyager spacecraft captured images of those same satellites. From left to right are Ganymede, Europa, Io, and Callisto.

An incredibly complex and sensitive machine such as LIGO takes a long time to build and develop. Construction began in 1994. In September 2015, it had finally reached the sensitivity it needed to detect gravitational waves. There were only a couple problems left.

The first problem: no one had ever seen a gravitational wave, and some scientists weren't even sure they existed. The second problem: only very heavy objects can make gravitational waves, and many of those heavy objects had also never been directly observed. Black holes, for example, are very heavy objects, many times heavier than the sun. Not one had ever been directly seen. What if they didn't really exist? Or what if they existed but were so rare that they would be difficult to see?

Remember, just like every other type of wave, a gravitational wave is a disturbance in the equilibrium. A black hole sitting all by itself is in balance. Black holes would only create gravitational waves if they were doing something that created an imbalance. Something, for example, like whirling around another black hole or two black holes crashing together. But how often could something like that happen?

So, there it was, September 2015, and LIGO was almost ready to officially start gathering data. It was operating, but the official "grand opening" hadn't happened yet. And in the early morning hours of September 14, LIGO detected a signal.[2]

If a pebble gets tossed into a pond, a floating fish bobber detector would see a pattern of up and down motion in the water. It would be a different pattern if an osprey dove in to catch a fish or if a motorboat zipped by. By looking at the patterns in the amplitude and frequency of the water height measurements, it would be possible to figure out which of those events was responsible for the wave.

The same thing happens with LIGO. The pattern indicates what type of event was responsible. But it's not easy to match the pattern to the event. So the LIGO scientists took some time to look at the signal, to make sure everything was working and it wasn't a mistake, and to figure out what the pattern matched.

The answer was amazing. LIGO had detected two incredibly heavy black holes whirling around each other, spinning faster and faster, and finally crashing together to make one much

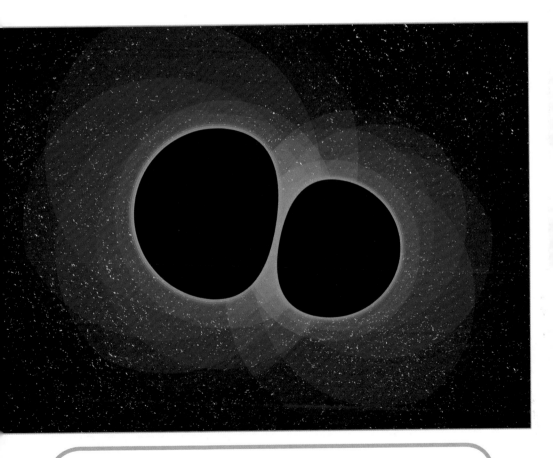

Gravitational waves are very weak, unless the objects creating them are very heavy. The first gravitational waves ever directly detected on Earth were created by some of the heaviest objects in the universe: two massive black holes.

heavier black hole. For the first time ever, waves (of any sort) had been detected from black holes.

And what black holes they were! One was an amazing twenty-nine times as heavy as our sun. The other was even more incredible: thirty-six times as heavy as the sun. In that one detection, gravitational waves were found for the first time (adding one more proof to Einstein's theory of general relativity), black

MAKING HEAVY OBJECTS

Stars come in many sizes, from about one-hundredth the mass of our sun to about one hundred times the mass of our sun. As stars age, their fate is linked to their size. The end of a star happens when it runs out of fuel. For stars lighter than eight times the mass of the sun, the end is quiet, something like when an ember in a fire dies out and leaves a piece of charcoal behind. Heavier stars end more dramatically.

Those stars are so heavy they collapse in on themselves, something like if that ember in the fire crushed itself down into a small diamond (although those stars, called neutron stars, are not bright and shiny). Even heavier stars keep collapsing even further to where they become black holes. Neutron stars and black holes are heavy enough to make gravitational waves—if they create some kind of disturbance in equilibrium.

holes were directly detected for the first time, and a previously unseen type of cosmic crash had been identified.[3]

Other Things to Be Detected

Any matter that disturbs the balance of space generates gravitational waves, but most objects aren't heavy enough to make detectable waves. That puts two requirements on a source of gravitational waves. First, it must be very heavy. Second, it must be imbalanced.

Earth is very heavy, but not heavy enough. The sun is about 330,000 times as massive as Earth, but that's still not heavy enough. It takes something even heavier, such as a neutron star, or even heavier, such as a black hole. Neutron stars and black holes are both objects that are so heavy they collapse in on themselves.

A neutron star or a black hole would be heavy enough, but they are not imbalanced when all by themselves. To create the necessary imbalance, the heavy object needs to be asymmetric in some way. A symmetric object is more or less one that looks the same from any side. A spinning neutron star, for example, looks the same from the front, the back, or the side—it's just a ball. If that same spinning neutron star has a "bump" on it, it is now asymmetric because it looks different from one side than it does from another.

Other arrangements are asymmetric, too. For example, two neutron stars whirling around each other are asymmetric. From one side, star one could be on the left and star two on the right. From the other side, star two would be on the left. From the front, both stars would be in a line. Sometimes a heavy star explodes and throws out a lot of its material in one direction. That is asymmetric also.

A neutron star is another type of very heavy object. A spinning neutron star could create gravitational waves, if it was uneven or imbalanced.

All those asymmetric heavy objects can create gravitational waves.[4] The frequency, wavelength, and amplitude of those waves are different depending upon how the heavy objects are moving. Asymmetric objects that are calmly spinning around themselves or around each other create continuous waves. An uneven explosion can create a "burst" gravitational wave. Two orbiting objects that spin closer and faster and eventually slam into each other create an inspiralling gravitational wave. LIGO's first detection was of an inspiral gravitational wave.[5]

LIGO has already detected a handful of other cosmic crashes, events that could never have been detected with other waves.[6] LIGO has many more future discoveries ahead of it, discoveries that will help build a more complete picture of the universe. In addition, the success of LIGO has given new energy to the efforts to build even more sensitive gravitational wave detectors. Those new detectors will take many years to design and build, and the people who build them will face many challenges. But those people will also celebrate the triumph of adding to human knowledge of the universe.

CHAPTER NOTES

Chapter 1.
What Is a Wave?

1. University of Utah, "Waves," ASPIRE (Astrophysics Science Project Integrating Research and Education), 2012, http://aspire.cosmic-ray.org/Labs/WaveBasics/waves.htm.
2. Julian L. Davis, *Mathematics of Wave Propagation* (Princeton, NJ: Princeton University Press, 2000), pp. 11–19.
3. Roger Knobel, *An Introduction to the Mathematical Theory of Waves* (Providence, RI: American Mathematical Society, 2000), pp. 3–27

Chapter 2.
Getting on the Right Wavelength

1. Chris Woodford, "Sound," Explain That Stuff, updated February 20, 2018, http://www.explainthatstuff.com/sound.html.
2. Carleigh Samson, Stephanie Rivale, and Denise W. Carlson, "Seismic Waves: How Earthquakes Move the Earth," Teach Engineering, updated April 11, 2018, https://www.teachengineering.org/lessons/view/cub_seismicw_lesson01.
3. Michael Fowler, "The Michelson-Morley Experiment," University of Virginia, http://galileoandeinstein.physics.

virginia.edu/lectures/michelson.html (accessed April 25, 2018).

Chapter 3.
Learning from Waves

1. Robert Grace, "Chapter 2: Where Does Oil Come From?" *Oil: An Overview of the Petroleum Industry*, 6th edition (Houston, TX: Gulf Publishing Company, 2007), pp. 52–54, e-book, Business Source Complete.

Chapter 4.
Gravitational Waves

1. John Dirk Walecka, *Introduction to General Relativity* (Hackensack, NJ: World Scientific Publishing, 2007), pp. 123–153.
2. Dennis Overbye, "Gravitational Waves Detected, Confirming Einstein's Theory," *New York Times*, February 11, 2016, https://www.nytimes.com/2016/02/12/science/ligo-gravitational-waves-black-holes-einstein.html.

Chapter 5.
Detecting the Barely Detectable

1. John Dirk Walecka, *Introduction to General Relativity* (Hackensack, NJ: World Scientific Publishing, 2007), pp. 241–261.

2. Peter R. Saulson, *Fundamentals of Interferometric Gravitational Wave Detectors* (Hackensack, NJ: World Scientific Publishing, 1994), pp. 9–27.
3. Muzammil A. Arain and Guido Mueller, "Design of the Advanced LIGO Recycling Cavities," *Optics Express* 16, no. 14 (July 7, 2008), pp. 10018–10032.
4. "LIGO's Interferometer," Laser Interferometer Gravitational-Wave Observatory, https://www.ligo.caltech.edu/page /ligos-ifo (accessed April 25, 2018).
5. Peter R. Saulson, "Interferometric Gravitational Wave Detection: Accomplishing the Impossible," *Classical and Quantum Gravity* 17, no. 12, p. 2441.

Chapter 6.
A New View of the Universe

1. Jim Quinn, "Stargazing with Early Astronomer Galileo Galilei," Sky and Telescope, July 31, 2008, http://www. skyandtelescope.com/astronomy-resources/stargazing -with-galileo/.
2. Govert Schilling, *Ripples in Spacetime* (Cambridge, MA: Belknap Press, 2017), pp. 186–205.
3. B. P. Abbott et al. (LIGO Scientific Collaboration and Virgo Collaboration), "Observation of Gravitational Waves from a Binary Black Hole Merger," *Physical Review Letters* 116, no. 6 (February 11, 2016), https://doi.org/10.1103 /PhysRevLett.116.061102.
4. Ignazio Ciufolini and Francesco Fidecaro, eds., *Gravitational Waves*: Sources and Detectors (Hackensack, NJ: World Scientific Publishing, 1997), pp. 15–47.

5. "Sources and Types of Gravitational Waves," Laser Interferometer Gravitational-Wave Observatory, https://www.ligo.caltech.edu/page/gw-sources (accessed April 25, 2018).

6. "Timeline," Laser Interferometer Gravitational-Wave Observatory, https://www.ligo.caltech.edu/page/timeline (accessed April 25, 2018).

GLOSSARY

amplitude The size of a displacement; waves of loud sounds and bright light, for example, have larger amplitudes than quiet sounds and dim light.

asymmetric Displaying an unevenness of some sort that makes an object or system look different when viewed from distinct angles.

detector A device that senses some quantity; ears and microphones, for example, both detect changes in air pressure in a sound wave.

electric field A way of thinking about the way charged particles are affected by forces from other charged particles; the electric field only exerts forces on positive or negative charges.

electromagnetic wave Changing electric and magnetic fields linked together; an electromagnetic wave will travel until it hits something that absorbs its energy.

electron A small, negatively charged particle that surrounds the heavy nucleus at the center of every atom.

equilibrium Balance; a system left all to itself—like a lake with no wind blowing or twigs falling—tends to reach equilibrium and stay there.

frequency The rate at which a wave goes from its maximum to minimum amplitude and back again, usually measured in hertz, or "per second."

general relativity Einstein's theory that describes how space, matter, and energy are all linked together; general relativity describes gravity as the effect of curved space.

interferometer A system that separates two beams of light and brings them back together; the brightness is a very sensitive measure of the difference in distance traveled between the two separate beams.

longitudinal wave A traveling disturbance in which the elements that carry the energy move back and forth in the direction the energy is moving.

magnetic field A way of thinking about the forces exerted by magnets on other magnets; moving charges—electric currents—are also magnets.

nucleus The relatively heavy positively charged particles at the center of an atom; the plural of nucleus is nuclei.

period The time it takes for one wave to complete one full cycle.

propagate To move away from a starting point in a specific direction.

seismic wave A sway or bump that travels through Earth; seismic waves can result from the disturbance created by an earthquake or from explosions or thumping against the ground.

sound wave A traveling region of high and low pressure, usually in air; the molecules most often move back and forth in the same direction as the wave travels.

speed The rate at which a wave carries energy; it is the product of the frequency and the wavelength.

symmetric Even or uniform, appearing identical when viewed from different angles.

theory A model of some aspect of the universe that accounts for observations and makes predictions about as yet unobserved phenomena.

transverse wave A traveling disturbance in which the elements that carry the energy move perpendicular to the direction the energy is moving.

wavelength The distance between one point on a wave to the same point on the next wave; for example, the distance from one crest of a wave to its next crest.

FURTHER READING

Books

Binney, James. *Astrophysics: A Very Short Introduction*. Oxford, England: Oxford University Press, 2016.

Clegg, Brian. Gravitational *Waves: How Einstein's Spacetime Ripples Reveal the Secrets of the Universe.* London, England: Icon Books, 2018.

Hall, Michael J. W. *General Relativity: An Introduction to Black Holes, Gravitational Waves, and Cosmology.* San Rafael, CA: Morgan & Claypool Publishers, 2018.

Hilton, Lisa. *Gravity, Orbiting Objects, and Planetary Motion.* New York, NY: Cavendish Square, 2017.

Negus, James. *Black Holes Explained*. New York, NY: Enslow Publishing, 2018.

Tolish, Alexander. *Gravity Explained*. New York, NY: Enslow Publishing, 2018.

Websites

American Museum of Natural History
www.amnh.org/explore/science-bulletins/(watch)/astro/
    documentaries/gravity-making-waves/
View videos and other resources that explain the physics of
gravitational waves.

**Laser Interferometer Gravitational-Wave Observatory
(LIGO) Scientific Collaboration**
www.ligo.org
Follow the LIGO collaboration as it uses gravitational waves to
probe the mysteries of the universe, such as colliding neutron
stars and black holes.

The Physics Classroom
www.physicsclassroom.com/class/waves/Lesson-1/
    Waves-and-Wavelike-Motion
Learn more about waves, including the various types and their
different parts.

INDEX